Elf-help for Busy Moms

Elf~help for Busy Moms

written by
Molly Wigand

illustrated by
R.W. Alley

ONE
CARING
PLACE

Abbey Press

Text © 1998 by Molly Wigand
Illustrations © 1998 by St. Meinrad Archabbey
Published by One Caring Place
Abbey Press
St. Meinrad, Indiana 47577

Library of Congress Catalog Number
98-74324

ISBN 0-87029-324-9

Printed in the United States of America

Foreword

Every "busy mom" knows this phrase is an understatement. Whether juggling a career and home life, or tackling the considerable feat of being a stay-at-home mom, mothers have a strenuous job requiring great reserves of courage, wisdom, and love.

When bogged down in the home trenches, a mom's patience may run thin, her good humor disappear, and her self-confidence crumble. And she may need a few nurturing reminders:

- You are a worthy and capable mom with a loving nature and good instincts.
- Raising children can be a source of great joy and inspiration.
- Your spouse and children share the responsibility for creating a happy home.
- Caring for yourself empowers you to care for your family.
- God is with you on the spiritual journey of motherhood.

Elf-Help for Busy Moms will bring these truths home to you, on even the most difficult days, and help you to discover anew the incomparable joy of being a mom!

1.

Be patient with yourself
while you become the best
mother you can be. Parenting
is a skill learned one experience
at a time.

2.

Affirm the right of every mom
(including you!) to make the
choices that are right for her.
Good mothers can be found
in the office and at the park.
We're all in this together!

3.

Ignore critical parenting advice from "well-meaning" outsiders. Trust your instincts about what's right for you and your family. Only you can see and respond to the complete picture of your children's needs.

4.

Resist the urge to compare
yourself to other mothers.
God gave this family to you
(and you to them) for a special
reason. You have everything
you need to be a loving,
caring mom.

5.

Laugh with your children.
Savor their sweet perspective.
Teach, through your own
example, the energizing power
of humor in a family's life.

6.

Make a point of giving (and receiving) more hugs, kisses, pats, and strokes. Look for new, simple ways to show love, acceptance, and encouragement. Kids need touch. (Moms do, too!)

7.

Allow your children the freedom to be different from you. Listen to their opinions and observations with open-mindedness and respect. Try to view their emerging independence not as a threat, but as a tribute to your parenting.

8.

Choose your battles. Expect resistance and rebellion as a child gains confidence and autonomy. Unless your child's safety is at stake, relax your need to control every action and outcome.

9.

Don't tie your self-worth to your children's behavior. Children, like moms, are imperfect beings. Love and accept their inevitable mistakes as stumbles on their journeys of learning and growth. Love and accept your own mistakes, too.

10.

Spend special time with each family member. Getting to know each other as individuals helps you appreciate and uphold one another.

11.

Understand that some moms are great with infants, while others are good friends and guides to adolescents. Look for the good in each age and stage. Children grow up so quickly. Someday you'll long for the time you're going through right now.

12.

When pressures build, and your children's demands take their toll on your good nature, ask God to help you control your temper. Take a time out. Count to ten (or a hundred, if need be).

13.

Create a partnership with your children's teachers and daycare providers. By combining your insights about your child's unique needs and attributes with the professionals' skills, your child's care and education will be a happy, successful adventure.

14.

Keep family communications open. Through family meetings, dinner talk, or casual conversation, encourage all to state their needs and concerns. Regularly taking your family's pulse can stop small problems from growing into unmanageable crises.

15.

While you're keeping your family talking, don't forget to express your own needs. It's easy for busy moms to become martyrs—working while others relax, cleaning up their messes, taking care of everyone and everything. Chances are your family will respond to your sincere request for help.

16.

Maintaining a pleasant and comfortable living space reduces stress and builds your family's cooperative spirit. Divide the housework fairly among family members. A happy family happens when everyone works together for the common good.

17.

Let the whole family help with meal planning, shopping, and cooking. Allow everyone, from preschoolers to teenagers, to share in mealtime chores. Preparing meals becomes more fun and creative when you're not doing it all by yourself day after day!

18.

Scheduling children's sports, lessons, and extracurricular activities can really keep you hopping. Add your own busy life to the mix, and days become overcrowded and overwhelming. Weekly planning meetings (and a calendar with big squares) can help you keep track of who's going where and when.

19.

Save time and energy for your marriage. The best gift parents can give their children is a demonstration of how to love and be loved. Connect with the people you were before you became parents. Rekindle your spark. Spend time "alone together."

20.

If conflict and negativity begin to take away your family's peace and harmony, seek help through counseling. Asking for help is an act of courage and strength. It shows your children that although you don't have all the answers, you're willing to work together to solve the problems.

21.

To nurture your children more freely and effectively, take time to nurture your own special needs. Treat yourself to a "day of luxury." Take time for a bubble bath, a manicure, a hair appointment, and a shopping spree. Pamper yourself and rediscover your natural femininity.

22.

Spending time with other moms offers you reassurance and support for your role as a mother. Have fun together. See a movie. Take a trip.

23.

Find caring, encouraging mentors by looking to experienced mothers for advice and inspiration. A woman who's been in your busy shoes can help you regain your perspective and enjoy these challenging times.

24.

Every once in awhile, indulge yourself. You deserve to enjoy life's pleasures. Whether your passion is for chocolate, shoes, or an afternoon nap...go for it!

25.

Resist the urge to fill up
your days with extra
chores, commitments, and
responsibilities. Schedule
some "down time" for solitary
daydreaming, reading, and doing
the things you love to do.

26.

Regular exercise and healthy eating will keep your life in balance and your problems in perspective. Take pride in the sensible lifestyle you're modeling for your family.

27.

Volunteering is great, but beware of becoming over-involved in time-consuming committee work. Reserve the right to say no. If, in a weak moment, you accidentally say yes, reserve the right to change your mind.

28.

Make prayer a priority.
Remember: God has lots of
experience handling wayward
children!

29.

Moments of solitude are essential to your mental health. Carve out a time and space where you can simply be you. Connect with your inner spirit and meditate to bring new strength to your daily life. A grounded mom is a happy mom.

30.

Don't let excessive worrying and anxious thinking take the joy out of motherhood. Fretting about your family's safety should not be a full-time job. Teach your children to be careful; then trust God to protect them when they're out of your care.

31.

You can cut down on materialism and simplify your life by helping family members differentiate between their wants and their needs. Instill the value of gratitude for the many blessings your family enjoys.

32.

Embrace the holiday traditions that brighten your life and enrich your faith. Let go of the chores and expectations that turn joyful occasions into stressful times. Focus instead on the simple activities that are most meaningful to your family.

33.

Spend time in nature. Gain wisdom from the phases of the moon. Watch and learn from mother birds and other creatures as they care for their own. Motherhood is nature at its most miraculous.

34.

Embrace motherhood as a privilege and your family as a precious gift from God. When a day feels too mundane to endure, think back on your life before kids. Acknowledge and appreciate the surprises children bring to each day.

35.

Expect the demands of motherhood to be rigorous, but remember that the rewards are bountiful. Your children are a joyful, hopeful bridge to the future. The seeds of love you plant today will grow and bear fruit for years to come.

36.

Take time to savor the memories you've created as a family. By viewing home movies, looking at baby pictures, and recalling days gone by, you'll nurture your family's sense of history and belonging.

37.

Make plans with your children. Talk with them about their future. Learn from their optimism and idealism. Anticipate the thrill of seeing them achieve their fondest hopes and dreams.

38.

If you cherish your children every day as the wonderful creations that they are, all the rest will fall into place. Love your kids. For love is what matters and lasts.

Molly Wigand is the busy mom of three children. She and her husband live in Lenexa, Kansas, where she juggles motherhood with her work as a freelance writer. She is the author of sixteen books, including four *Heavenly Ways* books, published by One Caring Place.

Illustrator for the Abbey Press Elf-help Books, **R.W. Alley** also illustrates and writes children's books. He lives in Barrington, Rhode Island, with his wife, daughter, and son.

The Story of the Abbey Press Elves

The engaging figures that populate the Abbey Press "elf-help" line of publications and products first appeared in 1987 on the pages of a small self-help book called *Be-good-to-yourself Therapy*. Shaped by the publishing staff's vision and defined in R.W. Alley's inventive illustrations, they lived out author Cherry Hartman's gentle, self-nurturing advice with charm, poignancy, and humor.

Reader response was so enthusiastic that more Elf-help Books were soon under way, a still-growing series that has inspired a line of related gift products.

The especially endearing character featured in the early books—sporting a cap with a mood-changing candle in its peak—has since been joined by a spirited female elf with flowers in her hair.

These two exuberant, sensitive, resourceful, kindhearted, lovable sprites, along with their lively elfin community, reveal what's truly important as they offer messages of joy and wonder, playfulness and co-creation, wholeness and serenity, the miracle of life and the mystery of God's love.

With wisdom and whimsy, these little creatures with long noses demonstrate the elf-help way to a rich and fulfilling life.

Elf-help Books

...adding "a little character" and a lot
of help to self-help reading!

Elf-help for Busy Moms
#20117 $4.95   ISBN 0-87029-324-9

Trust-in-God Therapy
#20119 $4.95   ISBN 0-87029-322-2

Elf-help for Overcoming Depression
#20134 $4.95   ISBN 0-87029-315-X

New Baby Therapy
#20140 $4.95   ISBN 0-87029-307-9

Grief Therapy for Men
#20141 $4.95   ISBN 0-87029-306-0

Living From Your Soul
#20146 $4.95   ISBN 0-87029-303-6

Teacher Therapy
#20145 $4.95   ISBN 0-87029-302-8

Be-good-to-your-family Therapy
#20154 $4.95   ISBN 0-87029-300-1

Stress Therapy
#20153 $4.95   ISBN 0-87029-301-X

Making-sense-out-of-suffering Therapy
#20156 $4.95   ISBN 0-87029-296-X

Get Well Therapy
#20157 $4.95   ISBN 0-87029-297-8

Anger Therapy
#20127 $4.95   ISBN 0-87029-292-7

Caregiver Therapy
#20164 $4.95   ISBN 0-87029-285-4

Self-esteem Therapy
#20165 $4.95   ISBN 0-87029-280-3

Take-charge-of-your-life Therapy
#20168 $4.95   ISBN 0-87029-271-4

Work Therapy
#20166 $4.95   ISBN 0-87029-276-5

Everyday-courage Therapy
#20167 $4.95   ISBN 0-87029-274-9

Peace Therapy
#20176 $4.95   ISBN 0-87029-273-0

Friendship Therapy
#20174 $4.95   ISBN 0-87029-270-6

Christmas Therapy (color edition)
#20175 $5.95   ISBN 0-87029-268-4

Grief Therapy
#20178 $4.95   ISBN 0-87029-267-6

More Be-good-to-yourself Therapy
#20180 $3.95   ISBN 0-87029-262-5

Happy Birthday Therapy
#20181 $4.95   ISBN 0-87029-260-9

Forgiveness Therapy
#20184 $4.95   ISBN 0-87029-258-7

Keep-life-simple Therapy
#20185 $4.95   ISBN 0-87029-257-9

Be-good-to-your-body Therapy
#20188 $4.95   ISBN 0-87029-255-2

Celebrate-your-womanhood Therapy
#20189 $4.95   ISBN 0-87029-254-4

Acceptance Therapy (color edition)
#20182 $5.95   ISBN 0-87029-259-5

Acceptance Therapy
#20190 $4.95   ISBN 0-87029-245-5

Keeping-up-your-spirits Therapy
#20195 $4.95   ISBN 0-87029-242-0

Play Therapy
#20200 $4.95   ISBN 0-87029-233-1

Slow-down Therapy
#20203 $4.95   ISBN 0-87029-229-3

One-day-at-a-time Therapy
#20204 $4.95   ISBN 0-87029-228-5

Prayer Therapy
#20206 $4.95   ISBN 0-87029-225-0

Be-good-to-your-marriage Therapy
#20205 $4.95   ISBN 0-87029-224-2

Be-good-to-yourself Therapy (hardcover)
#20196 $10.95   ISBN 0-87029-243-9

Be-good-to-yourself Therapy
#20255 $4.95   ISBN 0-87029-209-9

Available at your favorite bookstore or directly from us at: One Caring Place, Abbey Press Publications, St. Meinrad, IN 47577. Or call 1-800-325-2511.